The Open University

Visual Sources

This publication forms part of the Open University module A330 *Myth in the Greek and Roman worlds*. Details of this and other Open University modules can be obtained from the Student Registration and Enquiry Service, The Open University, PO Box 197, Milton Keynes MK7 6BJ, United Kingdom (tel. +44 (0)845 300 60 90; email general-enquiries@open.ac.uk).

Alternatively, you may visit the Open University website at www.open.ac.uk where you can learn more about the wide range of modules offered at all levels by The Open University.

To purchase a selection of Open University materials visit www.ouw.co.uk, or contact Open University Worldwide, Walton Hall, Milton Keynes MK7 6AA, United Kingdom for a brochure (tel. +44 (0)1908 858793; fax +44 (0)1908 858787; email ouw-customer-services@open.ac.uk).

The Open University

Walton Hall, Milton Keynes

MK7 6AA

First published 2010

Edited and designed by The Open University.

Typeset by The Open University.

Printed in the United Kingdom by The Westdale Press Limited, Cardiff.

The paper used in this publication is procured from forests independently certified to the level of Forest Stewardship Council (FSC) principles and criteria. Chain of custody certification allows the tracing of this paper back to specific forest-management units (see www.fsc.org).

ISBN 978 1 8487 3195 0

1.1

Contents

Plate I   Greece, Crete and the Aegean Sea, adapted from Morford, M.P.O. and Lenardon, R.J. (2009) *Classical Mythology* (international 8th edn), New York and Oxford, Oxford University Press, p. vi.

Plate II   Carlo Saraceni, *The Fall of Icarus*, 1606, oil on copper, 41 × 53.5 cm. Galleria Nazionale di Capodimonte, Naples. Photo: akg-images.

Plate III   Peter Paul Rubens, *The Fall of Icarus*, 1636–38, oil on panel, 27.5 × 27 cm. Musées Royaux des Beaux-Arts, Brussels, 4127. Photo: © KMSKB–MRBAB, Brussels.

Plate IV Pieter Bruegel the Elder, *Landscape with the Fall of Icarus*, 1560, oil on canvas mounted on wood, 74 × 112 cm, Musées Royaux des Beaux-Arts, Brussels. Photo: akg-images.

8

Plate 1.1   Red-figure vase from Paestum, southern Italy, showing a seated woman (possibly Phaedra), 360–350 BCE. Museo Archeologico Nazionale, Naples, 81855/H2900. Photo: Ministero per i Beni e le Attività Culturali.

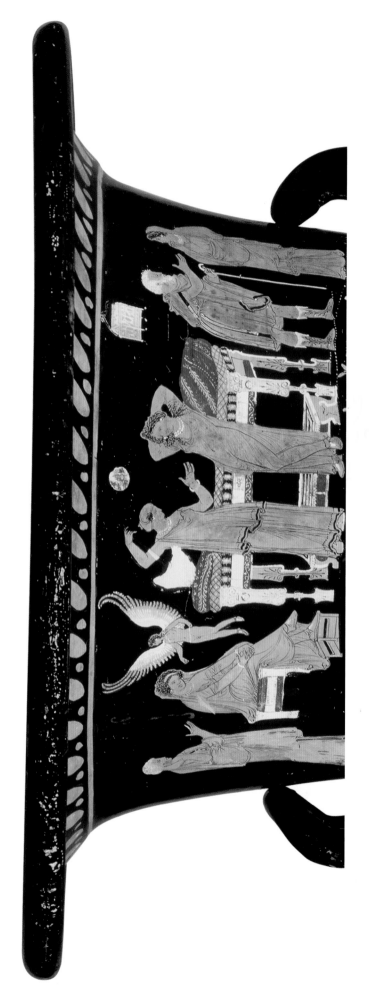

Plate 1.2   Red-figure calyx krater from Apulia, detail showing figures possibly from the myth of Hippolytus and Phaedra, c.350 BCE, height of krater 76 cm. Attributed to the Laodameia Painter. British Museum, London, F272. Photo: © The Trustees of the British Museum.

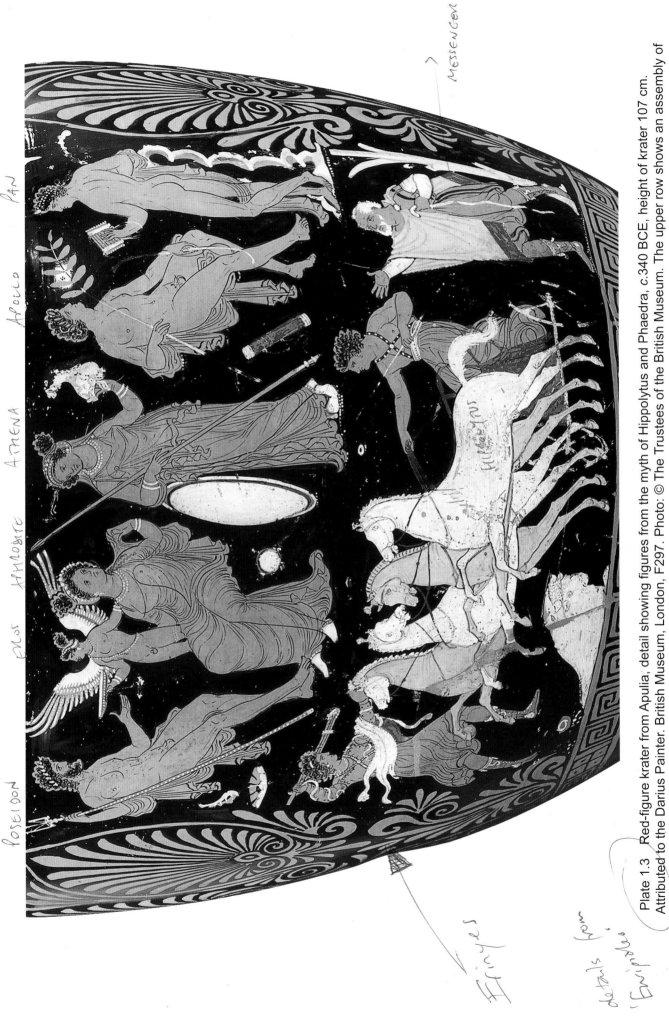

Handwritten annotations on the image:
POSEIDON
PAN
APOLLO
ATHENA
EROS
APHRODITE
MESSENGER ?
HIPPOLYTUS
Furies
details from 'Euripides'

Plate 1.3 Red-figure krater from Apulia; detail showing figures from the myth of Hippolytus and Phaedra, c.340 BCE, height of krater 107 cm. Attributed to the Darius Painter. British Museum, London, F297. Photo: © The Trustees of the British Museum. The upper row shows an assembly of gods, while below Hippolytus is startled by a Fury and a bull.

11

Plate 1.4 Wall painting from the south wall in cubiculum e of the House of Jason, Pompeii, showing Phaedra, early first century CE, 115 × 83 cm. Museo Archeologico Nazionale, Naples, 114322. Photo: Ministero per i Beni e le Attività Culturali.

Plate 1.5 Hippolytus panel from the 'Red Pavement' floor mosaic in House 2 at Daphne, Antioch, mid-second century CE. Hatay Museum, Antakya. Photo: Department of Art and Archaeology, Princeton University.

letter

after Euripides
after Ovid. (literary Roman form inspired visual art)

Plate 1.6   Wall painting from Herculaneum, showing Hippolytus and Phaedra, *c*. mid-first century CE.
Museo Archeologico Nazionale, Naples, 9041. Photo: Ministero per i Beni e le Attività Culturali.

Plate 1.7   The 'Red Pavement' floor mosaic in House 2 at Daphne, Antioch, mid-second century CE. Hatay Museum, Antakya. Photo: A Turizm Yayinlari, Istanbul.

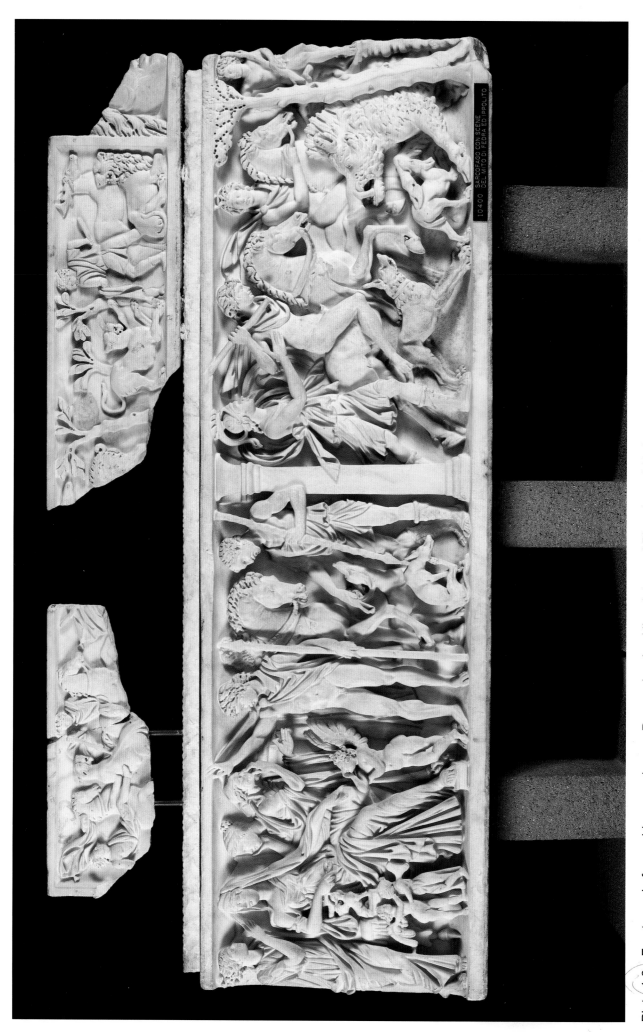

Plate 1.8 Front panel of a marble sarcophagus, Rome, showing Hippolytus and Phaedra, c.210 CE. Museo Gregoriano, Vatican, 10400. Photo: Vatican Museums.

10400 SARCOFAGO CON SCENE
DEL MITO DI FEDRA ED IPPOLITO

[handwritten marginal notes:] wealthy! who is buried. Elaborate, beautifully carved. Depiction shows sensation, leaving. Use of Greek culture to show a public education

Plate 1.9   Marble sarcophagus, Rome, showing Hippolytus and Phaedra, late third century CE. Museo Nazionale Romano, 112444. Photo: Ministero per i Beni e le Attività Culturali.

Plate 1.10   Ivory panel, part of the Querian diptych, northern Italy, showing Hippolytus and Phaedra, *c.* fifth century CE. Museo Cristiano, Brescia. Photo: fotostudio rapuzzi/Civici Musei di Brescia.

Plate 1.11   Ivory panel, part of the Querian diptych, northern Italy, showing Diana and Virbius, *c.* fifth century CE. Museo Cristiano, Brescia. Photo: fotostudio rapuzzi/Civici Musei di Brescia.

Plate 1.12   Silver plate, possibly from Constantinople, showing Hippolytus and Phaedra, 500–550 CE, diameter 25 cm. Dumbarton Oaks Collection, Washington DC, BZ.1949.6. Photo: © Dumbarton Oaks Collection, Washington DC.

Plate 1.13 Reconstruction drawing of a painting of Hippolytus and Phaedra, as described by Procopius of Gaza during the late fifth or early sixth century CE, in Friedlander, P. (1939) *Spätantiker Gemälderzyklus in Gaza*, Studi e Testi. Biblioteca Apostolica Vaticana, MAG, STAMPATI, R.G.Storia.III.3340(89), plate XI. Photo: © 2010 By permission of Biblioteca Apostolica Vaticana. All rights reserved.

Plate 1.14 Reconstruction drawing of a painting of Hippolytus and Phaedra, as described by Procopius of Gaza during the late fifth or early sixth century CE, in Friedlander, P. (1939) *Spätantiker Gemälderzyklus in Gaza*, Studi e Testi. Biblioteca Apostolica Vaticana, MAG, STAMPATI, R.G.Storia.III.3340(89), plate XII. Photo: © 2010 By permission of Biblioteca Apostolica Vaticana. All rights reserved.

Plate 2.1   Frieze from the Basilica Aemilia, The Forum, Rome (A)

Plate 2.2 Frieze from the Basilica Aemilia, The Forum, Rome (B)

Plate 2.3   Frieze from the Basilica Aemilia, The Forum, Rome (C)

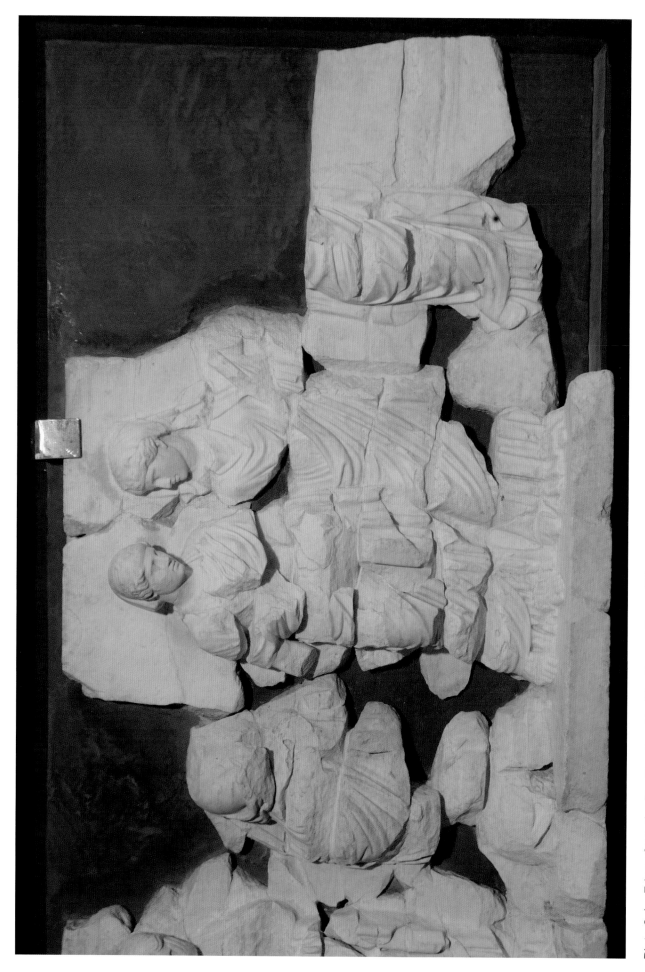

Plate 2.4   Frieze from the Basilica Aemilia, The Forum, Rome (D)

Plate 2.5   Frieze from the Basilica Aemilia, The Forum, Rome (E)

Plate 2.6 Frieze from the Basilica Aemilia, The Forum, Rome (F)

Plate 2.7   Frieze from the Basilica Aemilia, The Forum, Rome (G)

Plate 2.8 Coin of Nero, Rome, obverse: Nero with radiate crown, reverse: Nero, laureate and in the guise of Apollo, 64 CE, copper alloy, weight 9.17 g. British Museum, London, GR 1899.0218.46. Photo: © The Trustees of the British Museum.

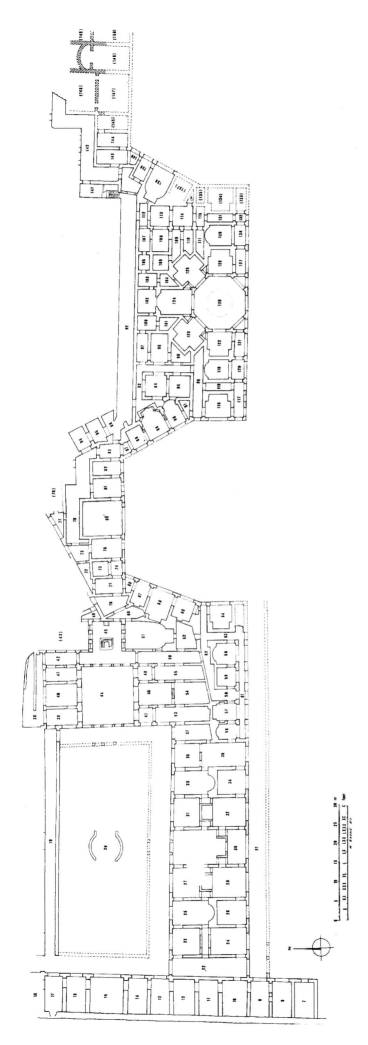

Plate 2.9   Plan of the Oppian Wing, Nero's Golden House, Rome, in Griffin, M.T. (1984) *Nero: The End of a Dynasty*, New Haven, CT and London, Yale University Press, pp. 134–5. Courtesy Laura Fabbrini.

Plate 2.10   Drawing of the decoration of the vault in the 'Corridor of
the Eagles' (corridor no. 50), Nero's Golden House, Rome, in Pinot de
Villechenon, M.N. (1998) *Domus Aurea: la decorazione pittorica del palazzo
neroiano nell'album delle 'Terme di Tito' conservato al Louvre*, Milan, Franco
Maria Ricci.

Plate 2.11 Scene at the centre of the vault in the room of Achilles at Scyros (room no. 119), Nero's Golden House, Rome, mid to late first century CE. Photo: Soprintendenza Speciale per i Beni Archeologici di Roma.

Plate 2.12   Scene of the parting of Hector and Andromache in the room of Hector and Andromache (room no. 129), Nero's Golden House, Rome, mid to late first century CE. Photo: Soprintendenza Speciale per i Beni Archeologici di Roma.

Plate 2.13   View of the 'Octagonal Room' (room no. 128), Nero's Golden House, Rome, mid to late first century CE. Photo: Soprintendenza Speciale per i Beni Archeologici di Roma.

Plate 2.14   Funerary altar of Petronia Grata, first half of the first century CE. Museo di Antichità, Torino, 535. Photo: Ministero per i Beni e le Attività Culturali/Soprintendenza per i Beni Archeologici del Piemonte e del Museo Antichità Egizie.

Plate 2.15   Inscription on the funerary altar of Petronia Grata, first half of the first century CE. Museo di Antichità, Torino, 535. Photo: Ministero per i Beni e le Attività Culturali/Soprintendenza per i Beni Archeologici del Piemonte e del Museo Antichità Egizie.

Plate 2.16 Altar dedicated to Sol and Luna by Eumolpus, a slave of Nero, and his daughter Claudia Pallas, 64–68 CE. Museo Archeologico di Firenze, 86025. Photo: Soprintendenza per i Beni Archeologici di Firenze. Eumolpus was in charge of the furniture in the Domus Aurea.

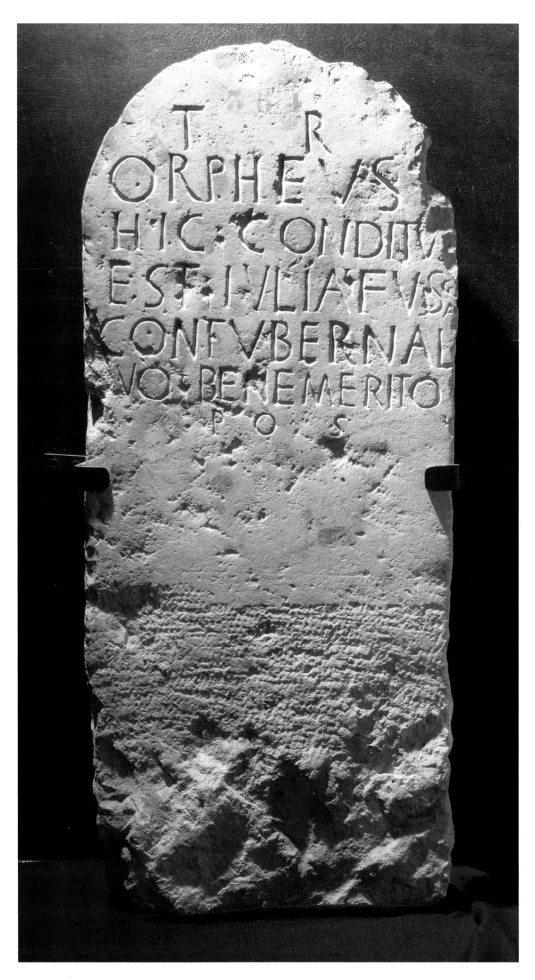

Plate 2.17   Gladiatorial tombstone of Orpheus, first century CE. Musée Archéologique de Nîmes, 365.
Photo: Dejan Stokic, Musée Archéologique de Nîmes. The epitaph reads: 'The Thracian [gladiator]
Orpheus lies here. Iulia Fusca set this up to her well-deserving partner'.

Plate 2.18   Marble relief from Halicarnassus showing two female gladiators, *c*. second century CE, 65 × 79 cm. British Museum, London, GR 1847.0424.19. Photo: © The Trustees of the British Museum. The inscription reads: 'Achillia and Amazonia fought to a stand off'.

Plate 3.1   Anish Kapoor, *Marsyas*, 2002, PVC and steel installation. Tate Modern, London. Photo: John Riddy. © Anish Kapoor.

Plate 3.2   Titian, *Diana and Actaeon*, 1556–9, oil on canvas, 185 × 202 cm. National Gallery of Scotland, Edinburgh, NG 2839. Photo: NGS Picture Library. Purchased jointly by the National Galleries of Scotland and the National Gallery, London, with the aid of the Scottish Government, the National Heritage Memorial Fund, the Monument Trust, The Art Fund and through public appeal, 2009.

Plate 3.3   Titian, *Diana Discovering the Pregnancy of Callisto*, 1556–9, oil on canvas, 187 × 205 cm. National Gallery of Scotland, Edinburgh, NGL 059.46 (Bridgewater Loan, 1945). Photo: NGS Picture Library.

Plate 3.4 Titian, *Danaë Receiving the Shower of Gold*, 1553–4, oil on canvas, 130 × 181cm. Museo del Prado, Madrid, P00425.
Photo: Prado, Madrid/The Bridgeman Art Library.

Plate 3.5　Titian, *Venus and Adonis*, 1554, oil on canvas, 180 × 207 cm. Museo del Prado, Madrid, P00422. Photo: Prado, Madrid/The Bridgeman Art Library.

Plate 3.6   Titian, *Perseus and Andromeda*, 1554–6, oil on canvas, 175 × 190 cm. Wallace Collection, London, P11. Photo: By kind permission of the Trustees of the Wallace Collection, London.

Plate 3.7   Titian, *The Death of Actaeon*, 1562, oil on canvas, 179 × 198 cm. National Gallery, London, NG 6420. Photo: © The National Gallery, London. Purchased with a special grant and contributions from The Art Fund, The Pilgrim Trust and through public appeal, 1972.

Plate 3.8   Black-figure lekythos showing the death of Actaeon (view with Diana), end of the sixth century BCE. National Archaeological Museum, Athens, A489 (CC882). Photo: © Hellenic Ministry of Culture/Archaeological Receipts Fund.

Plate 3.9   Black-figure lekythos showing the death of Actaeon (view with Actaeon), end of the sixth century BCE. National Archaeological Museum, Athens, A489 (CC882). Photo: © Hellenic Ministry of Culture/Archaeological Receipts Fund.

Plate 3.10 Red-figure amphora showing the death of Actaeon, c.490–480 BCE. Attributed to the Eucharides painter. Museum für Kunst und Gewerbe, Hamburg, 1966.34. Photo: Museum für Kunst und Gewerbe, Hamburg.

Plate 3.11   Attic red-figure bell krater showing the death of Actaeon, c.470 BCE, height 37 cm, diameter 43 cm. Museum of Fine Art, Boston, 10.185. Photo: © 2010 Museum of Fine Arts, Boston. Purchased with the aid of the James Fund and funds donated by contribution.

Plate 3.12 Metope from Temple E, Selinunte, Sicily, showing the death of Actaeon, *c*.460–450 BCE. Museo Nazionale, Palermo. Photo: © 1990 Scala, Florence. Courtesy of the Ministero per i Beni e le Attività Culturali.

Plate 3.13   Red-figure nestoris from Lucania, detail showing the death of Actaeon, 340–320 BCE, height 66 cm, diameter 48 cm. Attributed to the Choephoroi painter. Harvard Art Museum/Arthur M. Sackler Museum, 1960.367 (bequest of David M. Robinson). Photo: Junius Beebe © President and Fellows of Harvard College.

Plate 3.14 Roman gem showing Diana and Actaeon, first century BCE, blueish chalcedony, 1.15 × 0.90 × 0.20 cm. Staatliche Museen zu Berlin, FG 6435. Photo: bpk Berlin/Jürgen Liepe.

Plate 3.15   Marble sarcophagus, Rome, showing Diana and Actaeon, c.125–130 CE, height 1 m, length 2.35 m. Louvre, Paris, MA 459. Photo: © RMN/Rene-Gabriel Ojeda.

SARCOPHAGE : LÉGENDE D'ACTÉON
Environs de Rome
milieu du IIᵉ siècle après J.C.
Ma 459

Plate 3.16 Marble sarcophagus, Rome (detail from Plate 3.15, showing Actaeon)

Plate 3.17 Marble sarcophagus, Rome (detail from Plate 3.15, showing Diana)

The woodcut bears the labels **ACTEON** (top left), **ACTEON** (lower left), and **DIANA** (centre).

Plate 3.18 'Diana surprised by Actaeon', woodcut, in Ovidius Naso, P. and Regius, R. (1513) *P. Ovidii Metamorphosis cum luculentissimis Raphaelis Regii enarrationibus*, Venice, Joannes Thacuinus. Gerd Bucerius Bibliothek and Rare Book Collection, Museum für Kunst und Gewerbe, Hamburg. Photo: Museum für Kunst und Gewerbe, Hamburg.

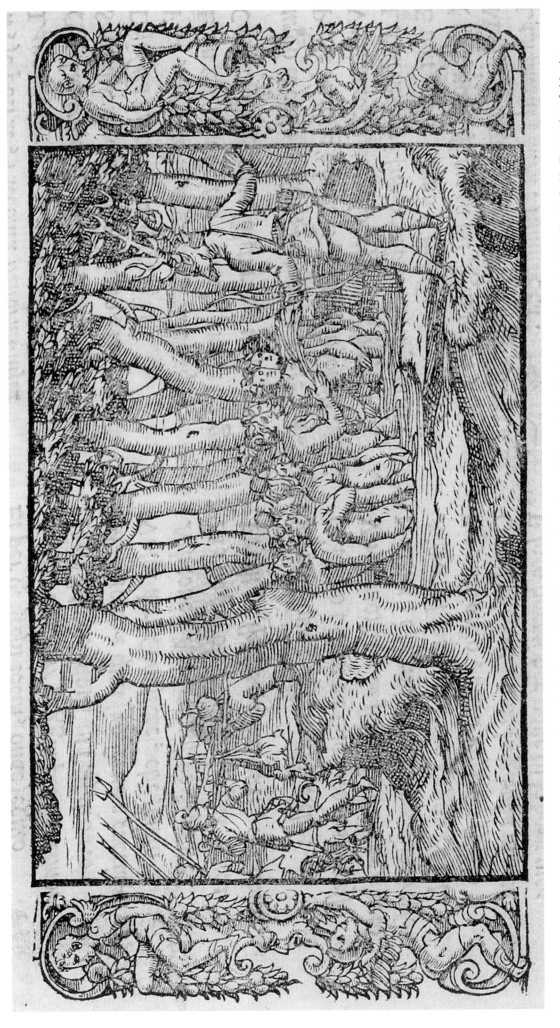

Plate 3.19 'Diana surprised by Actaeon', woodcut, in Dolce, L. (1553) *Le Transformationi di M. Lodovico Dolce: con la tavola delle favole* [with illustrations], Venice, G.G. de Ferrari e Frate. National Library of Scotland, [Ae].2/3/45. Photo: © 2009 The Trustees of the National Library of Scotland.

Plate 3.20 'Diana surprised by Actaeon', woodcut, in Salomon, B. (1557) *La Métamorphose d'Ovide figurée*, Lyon, J. De Tournes. British Library, London, C.107.c.8. Photo: © British Library Board. All rights reserved.

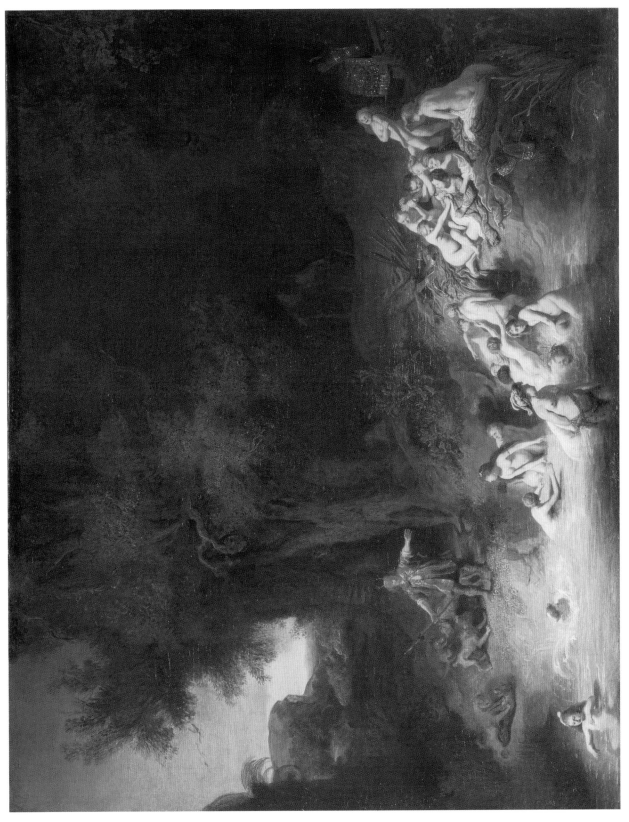

Plate 3.21 Rembrandt van Rijn, *Diana with Actaeon and Callisto*, 1634, oil on wood, 74 × 94 cm. Museum Wasserburg Anholt, Isselburg. Photo: © Artothek.

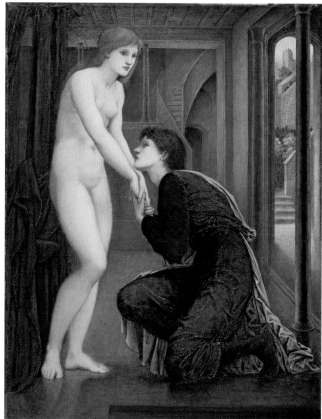

Plate 3.22   Edward Burne-Jones, 'The Heart Desires' (top left), 'The Hand Refrains' (top right), 'The Godhead Fires' (bottom left) and 'The Soul Attains' (bottom right), from *Pygmalion and Image* (Series One), 1868–70, oil on canvas, each painting 66 × 51 cm. Private collection. Photos: By courtesy of Julian Hartnoll/The Bridgeman Art Library.

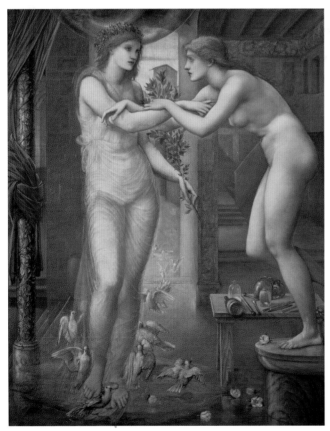
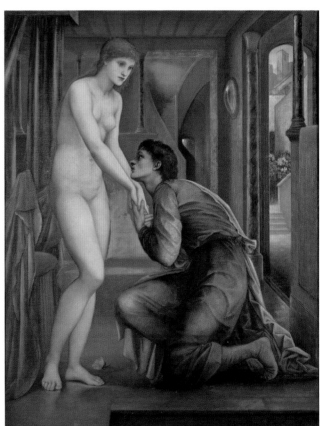

Plate 3.23   Edward Burne-Jones, 'The Heart Desires' (top left, 76 × 99 cm), 'The Hand Refrains' (top right, 76 × 99 cm), 'The Godhead Fires' (bottom left, 144 × 117 cm) and 'The Soul Attains' (bottom right, 99 × 77 cm), from *Pygmalion and Image* (Series Two), 1878, oil on canvas. Birmingham Museums and Art Gallery, 1903P23, 1903P24, 1903P25 and 1903P26. Photos: Birmingham Museums and Art Gallery.

Complete captions to the frieze images from the Basilica Aemilia

Plate 2.1   Frieze from the Basilica Aemilia, The Forum, Rome, showing a departure scene, first century BCE – first century CE, 75 × 190 cm. Antiquarium Forense, Rome, 3170. Photo: DAI Rome, D-DAI-ROM-dig2007.5976 and D-DAI-ROM-dig2007.5977. (A)

Plate 2.2   Frieze from the Basilica Aemilia, The Forum, Rome, showing a fight scene, first century BCE – first century CE. Museo Nazionale Romano. Photo: DAI Rome, D-DAI-ROM-dig2007.5868 and D-DAI-ROM-dig2007.0763. (B)

Plate 2.3   Frieze from the Basilica Aemilia, The Forum, Rome, scene showing the death of Tarpeia, first century BCE – first century CE, height 73 cm. Museo Nazionale Romano. Photo: DAI Rome, D-DAI-ROM-dig2007.2685 and D-DAI-ROM-dig2007.2693. (C)

Plate 2.4   Frieze from the Basilica Aemilia, The Forum, Rome, showing a marriage scene, first century BCE – first century CE, height 73 cm. Museo Nazionale Romano. Photo: DAI Rome, D-DAI-ROM-dig2007.2698. (D)

Plate 2.5   Frieze from the Basilica Aemilia, The Forum, Rome, scene showing the rape of the Sabines, first century BCE – first century CE. Antiquarium Forense, Rome, 3175/3176. Photo: DAI Rome, D-DAI-ROM-dig2007.8027 and D-DAI-ROM-dig2007.8028. (E)

Plate 2.6   Frieze from the Basilica Aemilia, The Forum, Rome, scene showing goddesses or personifications, first century BCE – first century CE. Antiquarium Forense, Rome, 3175/3176. Photo: DAI Rome, D-DAI-ROM-dig2007.8029 and D-DAI-ROM-dig2007.8030. (F)

Plate 2.7   Frieze from the Basilica Aemilia, The Forum, Rome, scene showing the building of the walls of Lavinium, first century BCE – first century CE, 75 × 159 cm. Museo Nazionale Romano. Photo: DAI Rome, D-DAI-ROM-dig2007.5859. (G)